17.56

Behind The Wheel™

Kyle Busch

NASCAR Driver

Simone Payment

rosen publishing's
rosen central®

New York

Published in 2009 by The Rosen Publishing Group, Inc.
29 East 21st Street, New York, NY 10010

Copyright © 2009 by The Rosen Publishing Group, Inc.

First Edition

Library of Congress Cataloging-in-Publication Data

Payment, Simone.
Kyle Busch: NASCAR driver / Simone Payment. — 1st ed.
    p. cm. — (Behind the wheel)
Includes bibliographical references and index.
ISBN-13: 978-1-4042-1896-3 (library binding)
ISBN-13: 978-1-4358-5403-1 (pbk)
ISBN-13: 978-1-4358-5409-3 (6 pack)
1. Busch, Kyle — Juvenile literature. 2. Automobile racing drivers — United
States — Biography — Juvenile literature. I. Title.
GV1032.B89P39 2009
796.72092 — dc22
[B]
                                                              2008018394

Manufactured in the United States of America

On the cover: Kyle Busch, driver of the #5 Kellogg's/CARQUEST
Chevrolet, sits in his car during practice for the NASCAR Nextel Cup
Series Pennsylvania 500 at Pocono Raceway, on August 4, 2007, in
Long Pond, Pennsylvania.

CONTENTS

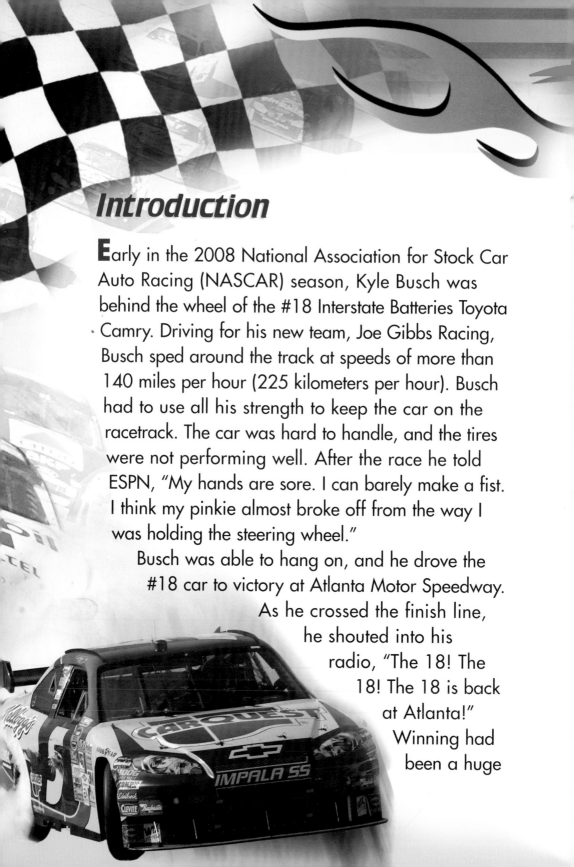

Introduction

Early in the 2008 National Association for Stock Car Auto Racing (NASCAR) season, Kyle Busch was behind the wheel of the #18 Interstate Batteries Toyota Camry. Driving for his new team, Joe Gibbs Racing, Busch sped around the track at speeds of more than 140 miles per hour (225 kilometers per hour). Busch had to use all his strength to keep the car on the racetrack. The car was hard to handle, and the tires were not performing well. After the race he told ESPN, "My hands are sore. I can barely make a fist. I think my pinkie almost broke off from the way I was holding the steering wheel."

Busch was able to hang on, and he drove the #18 car to victory at Atlanta Motor Speedway. As he crossed the finish line, he shouted into his radio, "The 18! The 18! The 18 is back at Atlanta!" Winning had been a huge

Kyle Busch celebrates his first win of the 2008 racing season at Atlanta Motor Speedway on March 9.

challenge. Busch told ESPN, "It was tough . . . [I felt like I was] driving on ice. It was the worst I ever felt in a race car, and I won the race."

The win represented several milestones. At age 22, Busch became the youngest driver to win at Atlanta Motor Speedway in Atlanta, Georgia. (His hero, Jeff Gordon, was the previous youngest winner. He won when he was 23.)

It was the first time a Toyota had ever won a Sprint Cup race. A foreign-made car hadn't won a NASCAR Cup event since 1954, when a car made by Jaguar came in first. It was also the first Sprint Cup win for Steve Addington, Busch's crew chief.

Because the Sprint Cup victory was not his only win that weekend, Busch added another famous first in Atlanta. He became the first driver to win both a Cup and a Truck event in the same weekend. Busch had won the Craftsman Truck race on Friday night. And Saturday, he had come close to winning the Nationwide Series race before his car blew a tire.

The win in Atlanta was his first victory of the 2008 season. But Busch had been on top of the Chase for the Cup standings for the previous three weeks. He hoped to stay on top for many more weeks to come. "Now that we've got the first one, you just try to go out and dig deeper and win more of them," he told the Joe Gibbs Racing Web site.

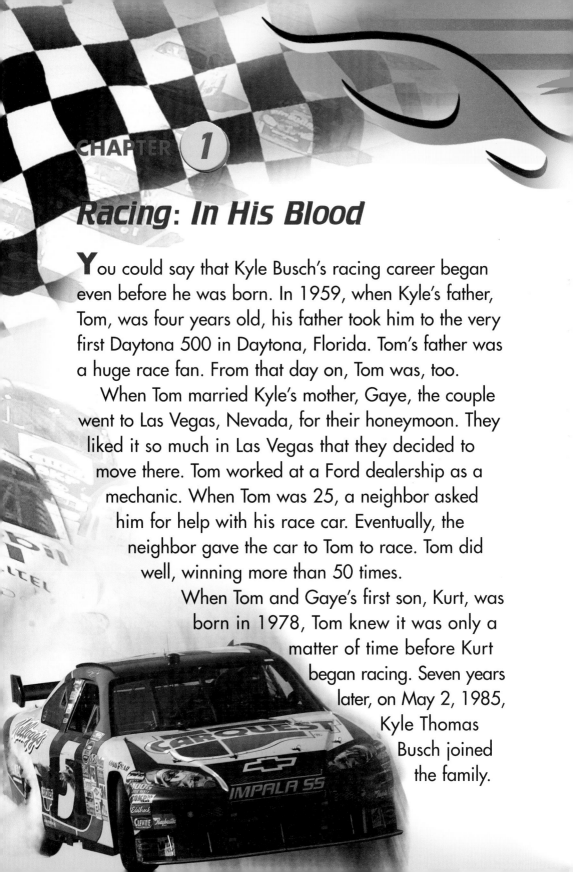

CHAPTER 1

Racing: *In His Blood*

You could say that Kyle Busch's racing career began even before he was born. In 1959, when Kyle's father, Tom, was four years old, his father took him to the very first Daytona 500 in Daytona, Florida. Tom's father was a huge race fan. From that day on, Tom was, too.

When Tom married Kyle's mother, Gaye, the couple went to Las Vegas, Nevada, for their honeymoon. They liked it so much in Las Vegas that they decided to move there. Tom worked at a Ford dealership as a mechanic. When Tom was 25, a neighbor asked him for help with his race car. Eventually, the neighbor gave the car to Tom to race. Tom did well, winning more than 50 times.

When Tom and Gaye's first son, Kurt, was born in 1978, Tom knew it was only a matter of time before Kurt began racing. Seven years later, on May 2, 1985, Kyle Thomas Busch joined the family.

In 2004, Kyle Busch's brother, Kurt, won the Nextel Cup Award, which he shows off here with his parents, Tom and Gaye.

Tom passed his love of cars and racing to both of his sons. Tom told *People* magazine, "Every hobby we had involved gasoline."

When Kyle was 5 and Kurt was 11, Tom built them a go-kart. Kurt raced the go-kart, but Kyle was only big enough to steer from his father's lap.

By the time Kyle was six, he was helping his father put cars together from spare parts. There weren't many other kids their age in their neighborhood, so both Kurt and Kyle spent a lot of time in the backyard garage Tom had built for their cars.

A Family of Racers

When Kyle was nine years old, Kurt started racing dwarf cars at the Bullring, a Las Vegas track (dwarf cars are smaller versions of American cars of the 1920s through

FAMOUS RACING FAMILIES

Kurt and Kyle Busch are not the first famous racing brothers. Ward and Jeff Burton; Terry and Bobby Labonte; Rusty, Kenny, and Mike Wallace; and Darrell and Michael Waltrip are just a few of NASCAR's racing brothers. One of the most famous racing families is the Petty family. Lee Petty won the first Daytona 500 in 1959. Lee's son Richard won an amazing 27 out of 48 NASCAR races in 1967. Richard's son, Kyle, is a current NASCAR driver. Kyle's son, Adam, was the first fourth-generation NASCAR driver. Unfortunately, he died in a racetrack accident in May 2000.

1940s). Kyle went along to every race and videotaped them from the top of the grandstand. Later, Kyle, Kurt, and Tom would review the race video. They would go over all aspects of the race. Kurt and Kyle learned everything they could about cars and racing technique.

Racing became a family activity. Most weekends the Busches would go to races. Some were on tracks in and around Las Vegas. Other races were in Arizona, California, or Utah. A few years after Kurt began racing,

Kyle began racing as well. He was just 13 when he began, driving in dwarf car and legend races (legend cars are miniature versions of 1930s Fords). Tom put a video camera in Kyle's car so they could tape the races. Afterward, they would go over every minute of the race, discussing strategy and driving technique and skills.

When Kurt and Kyle first began racing, they had only one car and one set of tires to share. Kyle learned the importance of taking good care of their car and other racing equipment. Everything had to last, or there would be no race the following weekend.

Both Busch brothers were successful racers. They knew a lot about cars and about racing. They also had the right mind-set. They didn't just want to win one race; they wanted to win again and again. They knew the way to do that was to focus on that weekend's race. But they also thought about the long term and made sure they and their car would be ready for the next week.

Competitive and Supportive Brothers

Even though Kurt is almost seven years older than Kyle, Kyle always wanted to do the same things as his big brother. Kurt never minded Kyle hanging around with him and following in his footsteps. "It was fun to have him around to compete with," Kyle told *People* magazine. "We never had any serious fights."

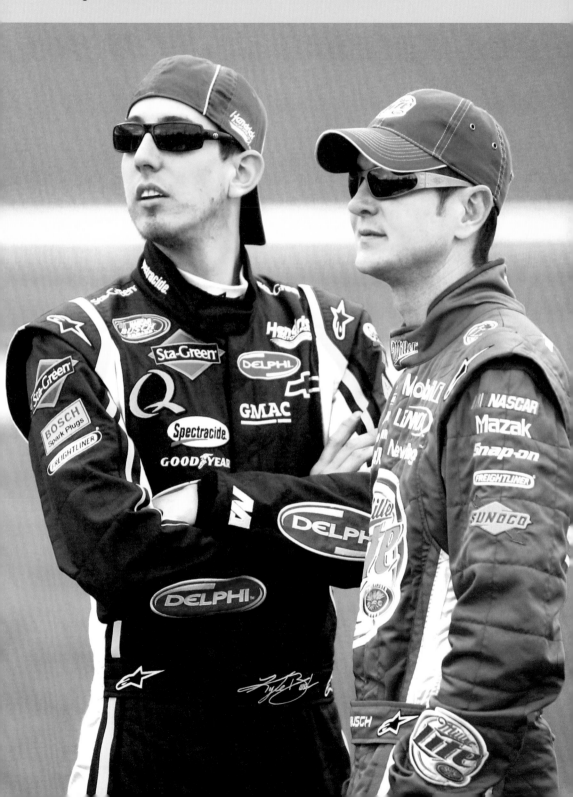

Kyle *(left)* and Kurt Busch check out the competition at a race in Las Vegas in 2007.

Both brothers say they are close—the whole Busch family is close. Kurt affectionately calls Kyle "Shrub," for "little bush" (a play on their last name). Their mother says that the boys were competitive when they were young, but they were also very supportive of each other. Kyle has always looked up to Kurt and continues to admire him. However, he admits that he also tries his hardest to be better than his brother.

Getting Serious About Racing

Kyle quickly became a racing star. By the time he was 15, he had won 65 legend car races. Kyle also raced modified cars. These are open-wheel stock cars with bodies similar to those of regular street vehicles. Kyle next moved up to racing late model cars. These are similar to cars driven in the NASCAR series. They are raced on dirt tracks and on asphalt.

When Kyle was 16, he won ten legend car races. He won so consistently that sometimes fans found it a little boring. They just expected he would win. The fans weren't the only ones becoming aware of Kyle's growing dominance on the racetrack. Companies who sponsor racers took notice, too. At the time, Kurt was racing for Roush Racing. Roush decided to sponsor Kyle to drive in a Craftsman Truck race.

During the 2001 racing season, Kyle Busch entered six truck races for Roush. His first truck race was August 3.

Eighteen-year-old Kyle Busch *(left)* poses with his legend car after winning a 2003 race in Las Vegas.

He did well, finishing ninth. However, because Busch was just 16, later in the season there was one truck race he couldn't enter. Marlboro sponsored the November 3 race that year at California Speedway. Because cigarette companies are not allowed to market their product to anyone under 18, Busch was not able to participate in the race.

Not a Normal High School Student

Kyle's main focus growing up was racing. Of course, he also had to go to school. Kyle did fairly well in school, although he didn't consider himself one of the smartest kids in his class. He tried to do all his homework during school so he had plenty of free time after classes. Starting when he was nine or ten years old, he would race home after school to work on his car. He would go immediately to the garage and slip his coveralls over his school clothes so he could get right to work.

Being so busy with school and racing, Kyle did not have much time for a social life. He didn't see a lot of the sights around Las Vegas or spend much time hanging out with friends. But that was just fine with him. The main thing he cared about was cars.

By the time he was 15 or 16, Kyle knew he wanted to be a professional driver. His mother tried to get him to consider other options, such as becoming an orthodontist. But Kyle was sure that he had the talent and determination to make it as a NASCAR driver. He was so focused on his racing career that he decided to try to finish high school early. Kyle met that goal, graduating from Durango High School with honors in 2002, a year early.

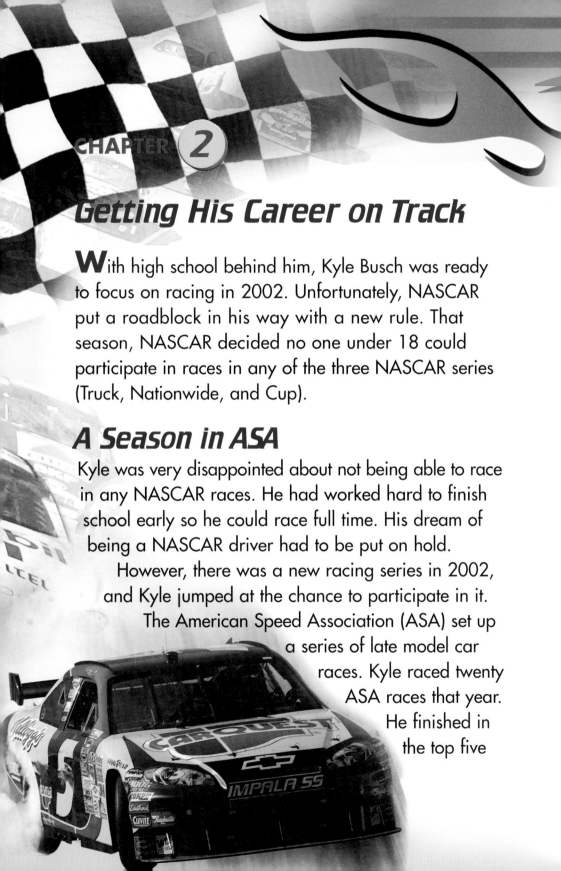

CHAPTER 2

Getting His Career on Track

With high school behind him, Kyle Busch was ready to focus on racing in 2002. Unfortunately, NASCAR put a roadblock in his way with a new rule. That season, NASCAR decided no one under 18 could participate in races in any of the three NASCAR series (Truck, Nationwide, and Cup).

A Season in ASA

Kyle was very disappointed about not being able to race in any NASCAR races. He had worked hard to finish school early so he could race full time. His dream of being a NASCAR driver had to be put on hold.

However, there was a new racing series in 2002, and Kyle jumped at the chance to participate in it. The American Speed Association (ASA) set up a series of late model car races. Kyle raced twenty ASA races that year. He finished in the top five in five of the races and in the top ten in ten other races. He finished the season in eighth place in the standings.

Looking back on the delay of his start in NASCAR, Busch agrees that it was a good thing for him. It gave him additional driving experience. He admitted to Dave Rodman of NASCAR.com, "It actually was better for me than what I planned it to be."

A New Home

Roush Racing had sponsored Kyle in some races of his early career. Kurt was racing for Roush as well, and Kyle often felt that he was known only as Kurt's little brother. Kyle wanted to join a racing team of his own. At the beginning of the next racing season, on February 4, 2003, Busch signed an agreement with the Hendrick Motorsports team. He described his switch to Hendrick to Lee Montgomery of NASCAR.com: "[At Roush] everybody knew me as Kurt's younger brother. Once I got to Hendrick . . . I was known at the racetracks as my own person, as Kyle."

Although Kyle had switched teams, he was still in Kurt's shadow. Over the years, Kurt had developed a reputation that wasn't necessarily good. He had gotten into fights with other drivers, and not all fans appreciated Kurt's style. So, at Kyle's first Busch Series race (now known as the Nationwide Series) in May 2003 at Lowe's Motor Speedway in Concord, North Carolina, fans booed him when he was introduced. "Probably not one person in

Pictured here in the #87 car, Busch runs a close second to leader Matt Kenseth during his first NASCAR Busch Series race.

the crowd had ever even seen me before, and I got booed simply because of my last name," he told *Sports Illustrated*. "Right then, I knew I had an uphill battle on my hands."

Despite being booed before the race, Kyle's debut in the Busch Series was a good one: he finished second. During the 2003 season, Kyle raced in six more Busch Series races. He came in second in one of them and in the top ten in three others.

In addition to the seven Busch Series races, Kyle entered some ARCA races. ARCA stands for Automobile Racing Club of America and is a series similar to NASCAR. Often, ARCA racers use the same types of cars and same tracks as NASCAR. Racing in the ARCA series gave Kyle another way to gain experience that could help advance his NASCAR career. Kyle won two ARCA races that year.

A Full Year in the Busch Series

During his few months off after the 2003 season, Busch was already looking forward to the 2004 season. It would be his first full season racing in the Busch Series. Although Busch had already had success in many professional races, he was just 18 years old at the start of the 2004 racing season. His goal at the beginning of the season wasn't necessarily to win the Busch Series championship. He was shooting for Rookie of the Year honors and a possible finish in the top ten in points. In 2004, Busch

A NASCAR driver couldn't get along without his crew. The crew chief is in charge of keeping the race cars in top shape, managing the pit crew, and working with the driver on race-day strategy. The crew chief stays in constant contact with the driver before and during the race.

During a race, only seven pit crew members can be in the pit during a stop. The jack man raises the car so tires can be changed. Two tire changers take off old tires and put on new ones. Two crew members carry the 80-pound (36 kilogram) tires to and from the car. Two more crew members fuel up the car. One opens a vent in the back of the car so the other can add the fuel. The pit crew performs all these tasks in just 12 to 14 seconds.

drove the #5 Chevy, and Lowe's was his sponsor for the Busch Series races. Lance McGrew was his crew chief.

Busch opened 2004 with an ARCA race at Daytona International Speedway in Daytona, Florida. The race was a kind of warm-up for the regular season, and Busch won the race. His first Busch Series race of the season was also at Daytona. Busch finished 24th but had the best finish of the four rookies in the race.

Plans for the 2004 season called for Busch to race in all Busch Series races. However, he was also going to be starting in a few Nextel Cup (now called the Sprint Cup) races. His first Cup race was in his hometown, at the Las Vegas Motor Speedway, on March 7. One of the most exciting parts of starting in a Cup race was that he would be racing on the same track as his older brother. Busch had an accident during the race and finished 41st, but he was excited just to be in a Cup Series race.

Busch's first win in the Busch Series came in May, when he won at Richmond International Speedway, in Richmond, Virginia. He not only won the race but also took over the lead in points toward winning the Busch Series Cup. Two weeks later, Busch won again at Lowe's Motor Speedway in Charlotte, North Carolina. Two weeks after that, he led the race in Nashville, Tennessee—until he ran out of gas with just four laps to go. He came back with yet another win the next week, at Kentucky Speedway. He had slipped to second in points after his problems in Nashville. Still, Busch was off to an excellent start.

The good results did not continue through the rest of June and July, however. Busch had a series of problems and did not finish in the top ten. He was not too worried or upset during this time. He felt sure that he and his

During the 2004 racing season, Busch drove the #5 car for Hendrick Motorsports and was sponsored by Lowe's.

racing team would figure things out. Rick Hendrick, owner of the Hendrick Motorsports team, remained calm also. Hendrick assured Busch that he wasn't going to lose his spot on the racing team.

By early August, Busch regained his earlier form and won at Indianapolis Raceway Park in Indianapolis, Indiana. The very next race, he won again and was second in points in the chase for the Busch Series Cup. With a third-place finish in the next race and ninth in the one after that, Busch stayed in second place in the Cup standings. He was thrilled and was having a blast. "I'm with a great team, with a chance to live my dream and a chance to win a championship," he told the *Sporting News*.

Busch went on to finish in the top five or top ten in almost all of the rest of the races in the 2004 season. At the end of the season, he easily won Busch Series Rookie of the Year honors. At 19 years old, he was the youngest Rookie of the Year winner in Busch Series history.

Another Busch was also successful that season: Kurt won the Nextel Cup. Kyle was the first to reach Kurt's car to congratulate him on his win after the last race of the season. Both brothers looked forward to competing against each other in the 2005 Cup season.

CHAPTER 3

The Big Time

After a very successful first season in the Busch Series, Kyle Busch was ready to tackle the Nextel Cup Series. His ambitious plan for 2005 was to race in all Cup Series races, in addition to Truck and Busch Series races.

A Full-Time Race for the Cup

Busch had already raced in some Nextel Cup Series races, but 2005 was his first year racing full time in NASCAR's most prestigious series. So, the 19-year-old Busch was considered a Cup Series rookie. He was the youngest driver in the series. He continued to drive for Hendrick Motorsports in the #5 Chevy. His sponsor was Kellogg's, and Alan Gustafson was his crew chief.

Busch's 2005 season got off to a good start. In the third weekend of the season, he won the qualifying race in Fontana, California. He set a track record of 188.245 miles per hour (302.951 km per hour).

Busch Series races are usually held the day before a Cup Series race. Kyle Busch is pictured here at a Busch Series race at the Las Vegas Motor Speedway.

Winning the qualifying race meant he would start Sunday's race in first place, called pole position. Although Busch started first, he finished Sunday's race in 23rd place.

The next weekend, races were held in Busch's hometown, Las Vegas. Busch finished 11th in Saturday's Busch Series race. In Sunday's Cup race, Busch started tenth. He finished in in second place. Busch told *AutoWeek,* "The race was a lot of fun, and I hope it wasn't a fluke . . . I can't say it's bigger than any of my Busch Series victories, but it's up there." Not only did Busch finish just out of the top spot, but he also beat his brother. Kurt finished third, right behind Kyle.

Having two sons in the Cup Series was thrilling for Tom and Gaye Busch. Tom told the *New York Times*, "Every day is Father's Day for me, I guess." Gaye was surprised and proud to see her sons doing so well. "Everyone always said they had talent, but we never believed it would be anything this big," she admitted to *People* magazine. Kurt, too, praised Kyle, telling the *New York Times*, "The kid's awesome. The kid's got better skills than I do."

Throughout the spring and into the summer of 2005, Kyle finished in the top ten of several Cup Series races. He won two Truck Series races and placed second in another. Busch also won a Busch Series race at the end of May.

Racing in three different NASCAR series was exciting, but it also required extra work. The major difference between the Busch and Cup Series races is the cars, especially the spoilers and tires. Busch had had plenty of experience with Busch Series cars the year before. It took him a few Cup Series races to get used to how the Cup car performed. He had to be able to tell his crew what to fix or fine-tune to make the car run at top performance. All of his experience working on cars in his backyard garage when he was younger was now paying off.

Busch's First Cup Win, and a Big Award

On September 4, Busch won his first Cup race, the Sony HD 500 at California Speedway, in dramatic, nail-biting fashion. During the last few laps of the race, Busch came into the pit during a caution flag. He sped into the pit fast and too close to the wall to allow the crew to change the left tires. Crew chief Alan Gustafson made an instant decision to change only the right tires on the car. This allowed Busch to head back into the race before the other drivers. Back on the track, Busch drove into the lead.

Busch's first victory might have been enough of a thrill, but the win was significant for another reason. With the first-place finish, Busch became the youngest driver ever to win a Cup Series race. He was only 20 years and 125 days old.

The following week, Busch finished fourth, and, at the end of September, he placed second at Dover International Speedway. At the time, Busch was 19th in the points standings. He had no chance to win the Cup that year. However, he and Gustafson decided to act as though they were in tenth place and did have a chance. They carefully studied other race teams and their strategies. Then, they tried to apply the best strategies to Busch's races.

Busch had two more wins late in the 2005 season. He won another Truck race in Atlanta, Georgia, on October 29. It was his third Truck win of the season. He also won his second Cup race, at Phoenix International Speedway in Phoenix, Arizona, on November 13.

Although Busch finished the season 20th in Cup points, he did win an important award: Rookie of the Year. There

Kyle Busch receives his Nextel Cup Series Rookie of the Year Award in 2005 in New York City.

was a whole week of events to celebrate his achievement, beginning with a luncheon at Lowe's Motor Speedway. There, Busch and the other rookies got to pull the yellow "rookie" stripe off their car bumpers.

The celebration continued in New York City, where Busch received the award at the NASCAR Champions Banquet. Busch gave a speech thanking his family, friends, and crew. He also thanked the other drivers in the Cup Series for their help and patience. He told them, "Every driver in this room has had that yellow stripe on their bumper. It's a year of making mistakes and learning from those mistakes. So I want to thank my competitors, who I consider the world's greatest drivers, for being patient and allowing me to be a rookie. Hopefully I've earned my stripes."

With his first year of Cup racing behind him, Busch was confident about the upcoming season. He was more at ease and more mature. He was still one of the youngest racers in the Cup Series, but now he had plenty of experience.

Sophomore Season

Busch's second full season of Cup racing looked like it would be another busy one, once again including Cup, Truck, and Busch Series races. Over the 2006 season, Busch finished in the top five ten times, including a win at Loudon, New Hampshire, on July 16. His impressive second season put him tenth in the points race at the end of the season.

Despite his many good finishes, Busch did have some trouble during the season. He was still dealing with being Kurt's younger brother. Since Kurt did not have the best reputation with other drivers or with fans, some assumed Kyle was just like his older brother and automatically thought he was difficult, too. Also, Kyle was much younger than many of the other drivers. He had to work extra hard in some cases to earn their respect.

But Busch brought some trouble on himself. In April, he got a ticket for reckless driving during a race weekend in Fort Worth, Texas. He also got a five-lap penalty for hitting Casey Mears during a red flag in an April 22 race in Phoenix. Busch and Tony Stewart got in several fights in the early part of the season. Busch was especially upset with Stewart during the Las Vegas Motor Speedway race in March. Busch even accused Stewart of trying to kill him.

Busch's biggest dispute in 2006 came during a race at Lowe's Motor Speedway in Charlotte, North Carolina, at the end of May. During the race, he and Casey Mears collided. Busch's car hit the wall and was wrecked. Busch was so upset that he threw his head and neck safety (HANS) device at Mears after the race. NASCAR officials could have suspended Busch for a week. Instead, they fined him $50,000, took away 25 Cup points, and put him on probation for the rest of the season.

Busch also had to meet with Mike Helton, president of NASCAR, to discuss the incident. The meeting actually proved to be positive. It gave Helton and Busch a chance to get to know each other. After the meeting, Busch spent a lot of time thinking about what had happened up to that point in the season. He had had a lot of disputes with other drivers. Busch realized that not getting along with other drivers would hurt him in the end. Busch told *Sports Illustrated*, "It's better to have friends out there on the track than enemies. In the Chase [for the Cup] that might

29

Many built-in safety features protect NASCAR drivers during crashes like Busch's 2006 wreck on this Charlotte, North Carolina, track.

not help me win the battles each weekend, but maybe it'll help me win the war at the end."

Busch matured a lot over the 2006 season. After a rough start, he settled down and focused on driving. Other drivers could tell Busch was learning more every week. Jimmie Johnson commented to *AutoWeek* that Busch had learned "when to push and when not to; when to be patient and when to be aggressive" He said, "He is learning as he goes and getting better with each race."

Changes Ahead

Busch's plans for 2007 were similar to those of the two previous seasons: racing, racing, and more racing. He

Busch holds the checkered flag to celebrate his first 2007 season win. He is still wearing his fire-protective suit, gloves, and HANS helmet.

would drive all Cup races, along with Busch and Truck Series races. Like the previous year, he would be behind the wheel of the #5 car for Hendrick Motorsports.

Busch started the season by finishing in the top ten in four out of six races. He also finished in the top ten in five out of the first six races of the season in the Busch Series, including almost winning at Las Vegas Motor Speedway. The first win of Busch's 2007 season came at Bristol Motor Speedway on March 25. That race was also the first one to use NASCAR's Car of Tomorrow.

After a smooth start to the season and a big win, some bumps appeared in the road. On April 15, at Texas Motor Speedway, Busch wrecked his car on lap

252 of the race. Busch thought the car would not be able to be repaired, so he left the track. What he didn't know was that his crew was able to fix the damage. When they had the car ready to re-enter the race, no one could locate Busch. Dale Earnhardt Jr. happened to be nearby, and he agreed to drive the car for the rest of the race. The incident was disappointing to the crew who had worked hard to fix the car. Busch was disappointed also and felt he had let his crew down by leaving.

During the early part of the racing season, Busch and Hendrick Motorsports were working on a deal to extend his contract. However, they weren't able to come to an agreement. Busch's problems getting along with other drivers—including other drivers on the Hendrick team—were part of the problem. Although Busch was generally on fairly good terms with other Hendrick drivers, he never felt like a true part of the team. So, in mid-June, he announced that he would leave Hendrick Motorsports at the end of the year.

The rest of the season was not easy for Busch. Because everyone knew he was leaving the team, he didn't get as much support from other Hendrick drivers. Busch worked hard anyway and had some on-track success. He finished second at Daytona in July, missing a win by just 0.005 seconds. He also won four Busch Series races and

NASCAR'S CAR OF TOMORROW

Early in 2006, NASCAR announced that starting in 2007, all drivers would use the same car in certain races. The Car of Tomorrow (COT) is a standard body that is designed to be as safe as possible. Drivers used the COT in several races in 2007. Starting in 2008, the COT was used in all NASCAR races. It is now often referred to as the Car of Today because it is used full time.

two Truck Series races. At the end of the season, he was fifth in points in the Race for the Cup.

In August, Busch signed with Joe Gibbs Racing (JGR), starting in 2008. Several teams competed to add him to their roster. Busch was most interested in JGR. Busch told owners Joe Gibbs and his son J. D. that he realized he had made some mistakes so far in his racing career. But he assured them that he would focus all his talent and attention on racing for them if they took a chance on him. They agreed, and Busch signed a three-year contract to race for JGR. He excitedly looked forward to 2008.

The 2007 racing season was difficult for Busch. He just missed out on a win in this final Truck Series race of the season in Homestead, Florida.

Off to a Good Start

For the 2008 season with JGR, Busch drove the #18 car in Cup races (referred to as the Sprint Cup beginning in 2008). With a new car, a new team, and a new crew, 2008 could have been a difficult racing season for Busch. But all of the changes didn't seem to affect him at all. He started his racing season with a fantastic first weekend. He finished second in the Truck race, second in the Nationwide (formerly Busch Series) race, and fourth in the Cup Series race at Daytona. After the second week of racing, Busch led the Cup and Truck standings. He was in second place in the Nationwide Series standings. Busch was pleased with his good performance. He told FoxSports.com that he thought he had "a great shot to win three championships."

Busch believes that part of his success in 2008 is due to his comfort on his new team at Joe Gibbs. He feels that he fits in better with his new teammates. One of those new teammates is his former rival Tony Stewart. Both drivers say they were worried at first about whether they would get along, but they have successfully put their past behind them. Stewart is very impressed with Busch's skills on the track and his devotion to racing. "He is amazing to me," Stewart told ESPN.com. "I'm proud to have him as my teammate." Busch has learned a lot from his teammates. Stewart is a mentor to him, and Busch and Denny Hamlin spend time together on and off the track.

Working with his new crew at Joe Gibbs is also a big plus for Busch. He trusts the team, especially his crew chief Steve Addington. Addington and his crew are just as happy to be working with Busch. "The guys love him to death. I believe they'd walk through fire for him . . . He's competitive and he wants to win races," Addington explained to the Associated Press.

Other drivers rave about Busch's excellent skills. Jimmie Johnson told *Sports Illustrated* that Busch has "a great feel for his cars and amazing car control. He can fly through the turns where other drivers will lift off the gas because they feel they're losing control. The kid is totally fearless." Richie Wauters is Busch's crew chief for Nationwide Series races. He thinks Busch could drive any type of vehicle. "Anything Kyle gets in, he has a chance to win. The kid is unbelievable, what he can do in a race car," Wauters marveled to ESPN.

Even though he has had many wins and excellent finishes, Busch is always reaching for more. "I don't win near enough to my standards . . . I want to be known as a dominant force in the Series," Busch told Eric Johnson of *AlpineStars News*. Busch realizes, though, that he is young and has plenty of time to reach his goals.

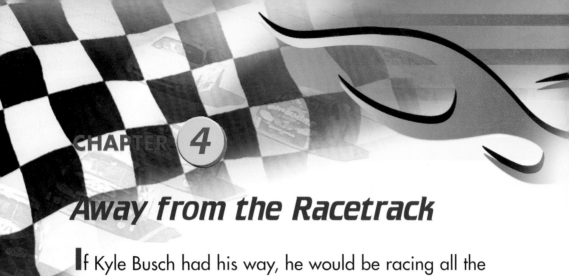

CHAPTER 4

Away from the Racetrack

If Kyle Busch had his way, he would be racing all the time. He hates it when he's not driving a race car. Keeping such a busy schedule racing in all three NASCAR series actually makes him more relaxed than he would be if he focused on only one series.

Home Away from the Track

Busch feels most at home on the track, but when he's not racing, he lives in Mooresville, North Carolina. Busch shares 126 acres of land with his brother. His parents and grandmother also live on the land, and they spend lots of time together when Kurt and Kyle are home. Busch's house is right on Lake Norman, and he has a pool in the backyard. Busch is not married but shares his house with Kelly and Suzie, his West Highland terriers. Not surprisingly, Busch enjoys cars even when he's not on the track.

Busch's dream car is this Saleen S7. It can reach speeds of more than 200 miles per hour (322 km per hour).

His dream car is a $600,000 S7 made by Saleen. Busch loves to drive cars in sand dunes in his downtime during race weeks in Las Vegas, Arizona, or California. He drives go-karts when he has the chance. Busch also races radio-controlled cars with Kurt and other drivers during racing season. When driving an ordinary street car on regular roads, however, everything about other drivers bugs him. Mostly, it is because he thinks they are driving too slow.

Busch likes alternative music. His favorite bands include Godsmack and 3 Doors Down. One of Busch's favorite movies is *Days of Thunder*, a 1990 movie

THE KYLE BUSCH FOUNDATION

During the busy racing season, Busch tries to make time to do charity work. In 2006, he visited a children's home in Michigan that was established for teens who have been placed outside of their homes. Visiting the teens at the home inspired Busch to start the Kyle Busch Foundation. Through the foundation, Busch hopes to help provide safe places for children to go if they live in broken homes, dangerous environments, or abusive family situations. The foundation raises money for children's charities around the country. Busch visits homes in race cities during the season and holds fundraisers on race weekends and during the off season.

about NASCAR. One of his nicknames is Rowdy, after a character in the movie. "Rowdy Busch" is painted on the door of the truck he races in the Truck Series. Busch doesn't follow other sports too closely, but he does like the Denver Broncos of the National Football League (NFL).

Chili dogs are Busch's favorite food, especially from the West Coast chain Wienerschnitzel. He also loves burgers from In-N-Out and anything from Baja Fresh.

Busch and team owner Joe Gibbs discuss strategy before a 2008 race. Gibbs was twice the head coach of the championship Washington Redskins football team.

A Top Performer

Busch admits that he's a bit of a loner. On the racetrack, he is aggressive and a risk taker. He's also all business when he is at the track. But people who know him well say that off the racetrack, Busch is a lot of fun to be around. He likes to play practical jokes on teammates and crew.

Busch always wants to be victorious but doesn't put too much pressure on himself to win every race. He prepares as much as he can, and then he lets everything fall into place. "As long as I know I gave it my all, I can't ask any more of myself than that," Busch told the Web site Race2Win.net. It seems likely that Busch will be giving it his all—and flying around the racetrack—for many years to come.

Glossary

asphalt A substance used for paving roads.

contract A formal agreement.

dispute Disagreement or fight.

grandstand Rows of seats where people sit to watch a sporting event.

mentor A person who provides advice and support, usually to someone younger.

milestone A significant or important event.

mind-set A person's approach or way of looking at a situation.

open-wheel race car A car that has wheels that stick out past the body of the car.

orthodontist A dentist who specializes in correcting the arrangement of teeth.

probation A period of time when someone is closely watched for any bad behavior or rule breaking.

qualify To meet certain requirements that allow someone to enter a race.

reputation Perceptions that people have about someone's character, behavior, or personality, which can be accurate or inaccurate, and based upon factual evidence and observations or gossip, slander, or misapprehension.

rival A close competitor.

roadblock An obstacle in someone's way.

rookie A beginner; a first-year participant in a sport.

spoiler A part on the back of a race car designed to help keep the car and its wheels on the track surface even at high speeds.

stock car A racing car that is similar to regular cars.

strategy A plan of action.

street car A car that is driven on regular roads instead of racetracks.

For More Information

Billy Ballew Motorsports
802-A Performance Road
Mooresville, NC 28115
(704) 664-7015
Web site: http://www.billyballewmotorsports.com
Billy Ballew Motorsports started competing full time in the NASCAR
    Craftsman Truck Series in 2002 and has had a variety of drivers
    over the years. The team has fielded competitive entries for many
    well-known NASCAR drivers, including Kyle Busch, Denny Hamlin,
    Bill Lester, Jeremy Mayfield, Geoffrey Bodine, Rich Bickle, Joe
    Ruttman, Bobby Gill, John Andretti, Martin Truex Jr., Andy
    Houston, and Shane Hmiel.

Joe Gibbs Racing
13415 Reese Boulevard West
Huntersville, NC 28078
(704) 944-5000
Web site: http://www.joegibbsracing.com
Former Super Bowl–winning head coach of the Washington Redskins,
    Joe Gibbs became a NASCAR team owner in 1991 and, with the
    help of his drivers and pit crews, has earned three NASCAR
    championships to match his three Super Bowl rings.

The Kyle Busch Fan Club
P.O. Box 1225
Harrisburg, NC 28075
Web site: http://kyles-corner.com/mainpg.html
An unofficial fan club devoted to all things Kyle Busch.

The Kyle Busch Foundation
559 Pitts School Road
Concord, NC 28027
Web site: http://www.kylebuschfoundation.org

For More Information

The Kyle Busch Foundation provides assistance to children's homes and the children who live in them.

National Association for Stock Car Auto Racing, Inc. (NASCAR)
P.O. Box 2875
Daytona Beach, FL 32120
(386) 253-0611
Web site: http://www.nascar.com
NASCAR, celebrating 60 years in 2008, is the sanctioning body for one of North America's premier sports. NASCAR consists of three national series (the NASCAR Sprint Cup Series, NASCAR Nationwide Series, and NASCAR Craftsman Truck Series), four regional series, and one local grassroots series, as well as two international series. NASCAR sanctions more than 1,200 races at 100 tracks in more than 30 U.S. states, Canada, and Mexico.

Roush Fenway Racing Museum
4600 Roush Place NW
Concord, NC 28027
Web site: http://www.roushfenwaycorporate.com/Museum/default.asp
This museum, created by Roush Fenway Racing, one of the leading NASCAR racing teams, includes historic race cars from the drag racing past up to the NASCAR present. It also includes a theater and interactive displays.

Web Sites

Due to the changing nature of Internet links, Rosen Publishing has developed an online list of Web sites related to the subject of this book. This site is updated regularly. Please use this link to access this list:

http://www.rosenlinks.com/bw/kybu

For Further Reading

Barber, Phil. *From Finish to Start: A Week in the Life of a NASCAR Racing Team*. Maple Plain, MN: Tradition Books, 2004.

Buckley, James, Jr. *NASCAR*. New York, NY: Dorling Kindersley Children, 2005.

Mattern, Joanne. *Track Trucks!* New York, NY: Children's Press, 2007.

Miller, Timothy, and Steve Milton. *NASCAR Now*. Buffalo, NY: Firefly Books, 2004.

Sports Illustrated. *Full Throttle: From Daytona to Darlington*. New York, NY: Sports Illustrated Books, 2004.

Stewart, Mark, and Mike Kennedy. *NASCAR at the Track*. Minneapolis, MN: Lerner Publishing Group, 2008.

Stewart, Mark, and Mike Kennedy. *NASCAR in the Driver's Seat*. Minneapolis, MN: Lerner Publishing Group, 2008.

Woods, Bob. *Earning a Ride: How to Become a NASCAR Driver*. Chanhassen, MN: Child's World, 2003.

Bibliography

Anderson, Lars. "Control Issues." *Sports Illustrated*, Vol. 108, Issue 12, March 24, 2008.

Anderson, Lars. "In It to WIN IT." *Sports Illustrated*, Vol. 105, Issue 11, September 18, 2006.

Bernstein, Viv. "Series Champ Now Bracing for Brother's Challenge at Daytona." *New York Times*, February 20, 2005. Retrieved April 2008 (http://www.nytimes.com/2005/02/20/sports/othersports/20busch.html?scp=1&sq=Series+Champ+Now+Bracing+for+Brother%27s+Challenge+at+Daytona&st=nyt).

Caldwell, Dave. "Kyle Busch Is Taking on the Present and the Future in His Bid for a Title." *New York Times*, September 23, 2007. Retrieved April 2008 (http://www.nytimes.com/2007/09/23/sports/othersports/23nascar.html?scp=1&sq=Kyle+Busch+Is+Taking+On+the+Present+and+the+Future+in+His+Bid+for+a+Title&st=nyt).

Joe Gibbs Racing Web site. "Kyle Busch—'18' Isn't Just a Number." Retrieved April 3, 2008 (http://www.joegibbsracing.com/2008/news_nscs/04_april/080401_kb_pre.php).

Johnson, Eric. "Being Kyle Busch." *AlpineStars*, February 25, 2008. Retrieved March 19, 2008 (http://alpinestarsinc.com/kyle-busch-feb2008).

McGuire, Bill. "Hooray for Hollywood." *AutoWeek*, Vol. 55, Issue 37, September 12, 2005.

Montgomery, Lee. "Conversation: Kyle Busch." NASCAR.com, February 26, 2004. Retrieved March 19, 2008 (http://www.nascar.com/2004/news/features/conversation/02/26/kybusch_convo/index.html).

Newberry, Paul. "Busch Beats Junior to Victory Lane." ABCNews.com, March 10, 2008. Retrieved April 2008 (http://abcnews.go.com/Sports/wireStory?id=4419177).

Newton, David. "Kyle Busch Needed More Than His Immense Talent to Nab Toyota's First Win." ESPN.com, March 10, 2008. Retrieved April 2, 2008 (http://sports.espn.go.com/rpm/columns/story?seriesId=2&columnist=newton_david&id=3285360).

KYLE BUSCH: NASCAR Driver

Pearce, Al. "Bet on It: Kyle Busch Will Win a Race Before the Season Is Over." *AutoWeek*, Vol. 55, Issue 12, March 21, 2005.

Pearce, Al. "Cup's Biggest Surprise?" *AutoWeek*, Vol. 56, Issue 34, August 21, 2006.

Pearce, Al. "One-Timer No More." *AutoWeek*, Vol. 57, Issue 29, July 16, 2007.

Race2win.net. "Race 2 Win's Q&A with Kyle Busch." January 23, 2004. Retrieved March 19, 2008 (http://www.race2win.net/qa/kyle).

Rodman, Dave. "10 Questions: K. Busch." NASCAR.com, January 11, 2005. Retrieved April 3, 2008 (http://www.nascar.com/2004/news/headlines/cup/12/27/kylebusch_10qs).

Ryan, Nate. "Teammates Stewart, Busch Forget Feud, Forge Friendship." *USA Today*, February 27, 2008. Retrieved March 5, 2008 (http://www.usatoday.com/sports/motor/nascar/2008-02-27-stewartbusch_N.htm).

Spencer, Lee. "Little Brother Cooled Down, Then Fired Up." *Sporting News*, Vol. 230, Issue 39, September 29, 2006.

Spencer, Lee. "'Rowdy' Kyle Busch Getting the Last Laugh." Fox Sports.com, February 29, 2008. Retrieved February 29, 2008 (http://msn.foxsports.com/nascar/story/7856120/'Rowdy'-Kyle-Busch-getting-the-last-laugh).

Spencer, Lee. "'Rowdy' Needs to Calm Down." *Sporting News*, Vol. 230, Issue 24, June 16, 2006.

Sports Illustrated. "Breakout Season for Busch: Busch Leads Points in Sprint Cup and Truck Series." March 19, 2008. Retrieved April 4, 2008 http://sportsillustrated.cnn.com/2008/racing/03/19/busch.success.ap/index.html).

Tresniowski, Alex, and Michaele Ballard. "Two for the Road." *People*, Vol. 63, Issue 14, April 11, 2005.

Wickham, Pete. "Two Good to Be True." *Sporting News*, Vol. 228, Issue 37, September 13, 2004.

Index

About the Author

Simone Payment has a degree in psychology from Cornell University and a master's degree in elementary education from Wheelock College. She is the author of twenty books for young adults. Her book *Inside Special Operations: Navy SEALs* (also from Rosen Publishing) won a 2004 Quick Picks for Reluctant Young Readers award from the American Library Association and is on the Nonfiction Honor List of Voice of Youth Advocates. She has also written about NASCAR driver Ryan Newman, 2008 winner of the Daytona 500.

Photo Credits